Monica Loat
July 2002.

Creative Assemblies

KS1 outlines on the life of Jesus

Heather Butler

Illustrated by Clive Edwards

By the same author:
The Grumpy Shepherd Christmas Plays
Meep comes to Earth
Pirate Party

Copyright © Heather Butler 2002
First published 2002

Scripture Union, 207–209 Queensway, Bletchley, Milton Keynes, MK2 2EB, England.
Email: info@scriptureunion.org.uk
Web site: www.scriptureunion.org.uk

ISBN 1 85999 466 0

All rights reserved. The activities and illustrations in this book may be photocopied for use. This permission is granted freely to owners of this book. This arrangement does not allow the printing of any of the published material in permanent form. Nor does it allow the printing of words or illustrations for resale or for any commercial use. Apart from this, no part of this publication may be reproduced, stored in a retrieval system, or transmitted in any form or by any means, electronic, mechanical, photocopying, recording or otherwise, without the prior permission of Scripture Union.

The right of Heather Butler to be identified as author of this work has been asserted by her in accordance with the Copyright, Designs and Patents Act 1988.

Scriptures quoted from the Contemporary English Version © American Bible Society, 1991,1992,1995. Anglicisations © British and Foreign Bible Society 1996. Published in the UK by HarperCollins*Publishers* and used with permission.

British Library Cataloguing-in-Publication Data.
A catalogue record of this book is available from the British Library.

Printed and bound in Great Britain by Creative Print and Design (Wales) Ebbw Vale.

Scripture Union is an international Christian charity working with churches in more than 130 countries, providing resources to bring the good news about Jesus Christ to children, young people and families and to encourage them to develop spiritually through the Bible and prayer. As well as our network of volunteers, staff and associates who run holidays, church-based events and school Christian groups, we produce a wide range of publications and support those who use our resources through training programmes.

Contents

Autumn Term

Spring Term

Summer Term

Enjoying ourselves

Jesus goes to a wedding

This assembly can be linked to the beginning of the school year.

Children will...

- talk about the contents of a lunch box and wedding items
- listen to the story of Jesus turning water to wine at a wedding (John 2:1–11)
- think about how God wants us to enjoy ourselves and, at the beginning of the new school year, how they can help that to happen

You'll need...

- 2 lunch boxes, one containing food, one empty
- wedding/meal items, eg menus, serviettes, pictures of food
- large jar (where wine was kept)

Introduction...

Talk about **lunch boxes** and their contents. Ask the children what it would be like to open the box and find it empty. Demonstrate using the lunch boxes.

Talk about **weddings**, the key people, reception, food, how long they last.

Story...

When Jesus was alive, weddings went on for several days and the whole village would be come to celebrate. There would be dancing and eating and it was really important for everything to run smoothly.

One day, Jesus was in a town called Cana and everyone, including him, was having a brilliant time at a wedding. We don't know what they had to eat, but let's have a guess. *(Ask the children what they think the people might have eaten.)*

But we do know what they had to drink: wine.

The problem was that the wine ran out! The servant lifted up the jar where the wine was kept, and it was empty.

Absolutely empty.

Not a drop left.

Now, if that happened today, we might go to the supermarket to buy some more wine, but the people at this wedding couldn't do that. Why not? *(There were no supermarkets.)*

It was awful. So embarrassing. The bride would have been upset. So would the groom and their parents and... they did not know what to do.

Until Jesus' mother got to hear about it. She knew something very special about her son. She knew he would not want the wedding to be spoilt and she also knew he could do something about it.

'There's no wine left,' she whispered to Jesus.

Jesus must have looked around and in the corner of the room he saw six stone water jars. The jars were very big, and when they were filled, each would hold about 100 litres. Jesus called some of the servants over.

'Fill those jars with water,' he told them. They must have wondered who Jesus was, but they did what he asked and filled them right up to the brim.

'Now,' Jesus said, 'take some water out and take it to the man who's in charge of the wedding feast.'

The servants did as Jesus told them, and the man in charge discovered that the water wasn't water anymore. It had changed to beautiful wine. Normally, people served the best wine first and kept the cheap, poor wine until the end. But not at this wedding!

Thinking time...

Jesus changed the water to wine because he wanted everything to go well for the bride and groom, so they could enjoy themselves at the wedding feast. He wants us to enjoy ourselves as well.
At the start of a new school year let's think about what we enjoy doing (eg being with our friends, enjoying our favourite lessons) and how we can make sure we carry on enjoying what we do (eg keeping healthy, eating the right food, being kind, sticking to school rules, working hard).
Which of these is most important?
Why?

Prayer...

Dear God,
Thank you that you want the best for each one of us. Thank you for our friends and families and all the other people who look after us and love us. Help us, at the start of a new year in school, to be like you and think about other people so they can enjoy themselves too.
Amen.

Song: Jesus Love is very wonderful.

Helping others be happy

Jesus heals Simon's mother-in-law

Children will...

- inspect the contents of a first aid box
- hear how Jesus healed Simon's mother-in-law (Luke 4:38–40)
- think about how they can cheer people up and make them feel better

You'll need...

- first aid box
- table and blanket

Introduction...

Explore the contents of a **first aid box**. First aid boxes like we have today did not exist when Jesus lived on earth. People used herbs for medicines, and they didn't have hospitals.
Discuss what other **medical facilities** we have today.

Story...

Jesus met lots of people who were ill. Here's what happened to one of them. Simon was one of Jesus' special friends who lived in a place called Capernaum.

Jesus went to his house one day and Simon's wife's mother was so ill she couldn't even get out of bed. *(Act out with child lying on table under blanket.)*

Of course, Simon's family told Jesus about her and asked if he could do anything to help. The first thing he did was he went and stood by her.

What do you think Jesus thought as he stood there?

What do you think Simon's mother-in-law thought?

And Simon, what was he thinking?

Jesus told the illness to leave her and straight away she sat up. *(Child on table sits up.)*

What do you think her face looked like? *(Happy, amazed.)*

And Simon's?

The Bible says that as soon as she was better, she got out of bed and made a drink and some food for Jesus and the others.

Well, everyone in the village got to hear about it. By the time the sun had set, they had all come to Simon's house to have a look. What do you think they said to each other?

The people didn't go on their own to see Jesus, either. They brought all their friends and their sons and their daughters and their mums and their dads and their cousins and anyone who was ill. And Jesus healed them all. The Bible says he placed his hands on every one of them and healed them.

That must have been one happy village. All those people who had been ill were suddenly better again, thanks to Jesus.

Thinking time...

When Jesus did something good, he must have felt really happy inside.

Are there any times you can think of when you did something really good?

What did it feel like?

Can you think of anyone you could cheer up and help to feel better?

Prayer...

Dear God,
Thank you that you can heal people and make them feel better on the inside as well. Help us to look after people, too.
Amen.

Skills we've been given

the parable of the gold coins

This assembly can be linked to harvest.

Children will...

- think about money and how we can use it wisely
- take part in the parable of the gold coins from Matthew 25:14–30
- reflect on skills the children have and how they can use them

You'll need...

- coins from UK and different countries
- plastic gold coins
- clothes for dressing up rich man and three servants

5 bags of coins.

Introduction...

Look at the **coins** and talk about what you can buy with them. What would be a sensible way of spending money? (Link in to harvest theme/giving to charity if appropriate.)

Story...

Jesus told a story about someone who was given some money. He just held on to it and did nothing with it.

The story starts with a rich man and three people who worked for him. *(Ask children to come to the front to act the story out.)* Now, the rich man was going off on a long journey, and before he left, he called these three servants to his office. He gave the first servant 1,000 gold coins. The next servant got 5,000 coins, and the third, 2,000 coins. Then off he went.

Now, the rich man knew the servants very well, and knew what they were good at. The servant who got 5,000 gold coins spent his money and made some more. He ended up with another 5,000 coins. *(Give more gold coins to the appropriate child.)* That man used the money sensibly.

The same thing happened to the servant who was given 2,000 gold coins. He went off and made another 2,000 coins.

But the man who had been given 1,000 coins dug a hole in the ground. Can you guess what he did next? *(Hid his money.)* He did not do anything with it.

Well, after a long time, the rich man came home again.

The servant who had been given 5,000 gold coins showed his other 5,000 coins.

'Well done!' the man said. 'I'm going to put you in charge of something really big.'

Next, the servant who had been given 2,000 gold coins came forward.

'Well done!' the man said again. 'You too will be in charge of something really big.'

Finally, the servant who had received 1,000 gold coins came in.

'I was afraid,' he said, 'so I hid your money in the ground. Look! Have it back.'

What do you think the rich man said?

'You bad and lazy man,' he said. 'Take the money away from him and throw him outside.'

Thinking time...

How do you think the rich man felt before he went on his journey?
When he came home?
When he saw each of the servants he had given his own money to?
How were the three servants who had been given money feeling?
Which of them had used what they had been given properly?
What have you been given – what are you good at?
How can you use those skills?

Prayer...

Dear God,
There are so many things we can do with our money and the things we are good at. Help us to use them properly.
Amen.

Sing: Give me oil in my lamp.
or Praise Him, Praise Him

Making friends

Jesus' special friends

Children will...

- think about making new friends
- learn about some of Jesus' friends (Matthew 4:18–22)

You'll need...

- some dry leaves
- net, toy boat, cut-out fish-shape
- blindfold
- labels for Simon, Andrew, James, John, Matthew and Simon the rebel
- paper and felt-tip pen or OHP
- coins
- cardboard dagger/sword

Introduction...

Talk about the sound **dry leaves** make when you walk on them. Link this to other things that happen in **autumn**, especially **making new friends** at the beginning of a new school year. Ask for a volunteer to be blindfolded and sit on a chair at the front.

Story...

There were two brothers in the Bible. One was called Simon and the other Andrew. Simon was later called Peter, but when the Bible first talks about him he was called Simon, so we'll call him Simon as well.

(Ask two children to come to the front to be Simon and Andrew and give them appropriate labels.

Ask the blindfolded child to guess what job they did from the clues they will be given. For example, they should feel the net, fish-shape and toy boat to guess 'fisherman'. The child can then return to his/her seat.)

As fishermen they would use their boats or stand on the side of the lake with enormous nets and throw them as far as they could to catch the fish swimming near the shore.

Then one day a sound was heard on the stones along the beach. *(Press down on dry leaves to make the crunch of footsteps.)*

Someone was coming. It was Jesus.

'Come with me,' he said. Simon and Andrew knew this was someone special, someone worth spending time with, so they left their nets and their boats and went with him.

They walked along the side of the lake for a little while until they came to some more fishermen sitting in their boat. James and John were there.

(Ask children to come to the front to be them.)

They left their boat and went with Jesus too.

Simon, Andrew, James and John wanted to spend time with Jesus. They wanted to be his friends.

Why do people want to be friends? Why do you like your friends?

Jesus had other friends as well.

(Ask a child to come to the front to be blindfolded. Play 'guess the job' again.)

Matthew was a tax collector. *(Use coins.)*

Simon was a rebel who fought the Romans. *(Use dagger.)*

They went with Jesus as well and became his friends. Jesus didn't mind what jobs they did or how rich they were or what they looked like. He liked them just because they were people.

Thinking time...

Who are the people you most like spending time with?
Why do you like them?
What do you think your friends like about you?
Do you know anyone who hasn't got a friend?

Prayer...

Dear God,
Thank you for all our friends. You looked after everyone and loved them. Help us to do the same.
Amen.

Role models

Jesus heals Bartimaeus

This assembly can be linked to 5 November.

Children will...

- think about fireworks and what it would be like not to be able to see them
- hear the story of Bartimaeus (Mark 10:46–52)
- think about people they 'follow' – are they good role models?

You'll need...

- used fireworks (carried in tin for safety reasons)
- blindfold
- coins, food, bowl, coat/cloak

Introduction...

Blindfold a child and take out a **firework**. Ask other children to describe what it is, and the sound it would make. Pretend it is going off and point out the bright colours and how exciting it looks. The blindfolded child can only hear things.

Story...

That is all Bartimaeus would have been able to do when Jesus came to visit Jericho. Bartimaeus was blind. He sat by the gates of the city hoping people would throw a coin or some food to him as they went by. He would collect them in his bowl as he sat on his cloak.

(Ask some children to come to the front to help act the story out.)

Well, one day, Bartimaeus was sitting in his usual spot, and most people were ignoring him as usual. Then he began hearing a name. People kept saying it. 'Jesus! He's coming to town. He's on his way!'

Bartimaeus must have sat up. He had heard about Jesus. He was the man who made people better, and he was going to walk past! There was only one thing for it.

'Hey!' Bartimaeus yelled. 'I'm over here.'

'Be quiet,' everyone around him kept on saying. 'He's not interested in you.'

'He is!' Bartimaeus said, and shouted even louder.

'Jesus! I'm here! I'm over here!'

Jesus was near now. Bartimaeus could tell because everyone was moving around him and saying things like, 'Look, he's coming!' There was only one thing for it. Bartimaeus took a deep, deep breath and...

Jesus stopped. Absolutely still. And the crowd stopped as well. And listened.

'I'm over here!'

'Call him,' Jesus said quietly.

(You could play 'Chinese whispers' at this point to get Bartimaeus if that is appropriate.)

So Bartimaeus was taken to Jesus. They had to calm him down a bit because, even though he couldn't see and might have hurt himself, he started jumping up and down.

'What do you want me for?' Jesus asked him.

'I want you to make me see again,' Bartimaeus said.

'OK,' Jesus said, 'because of your faith in me, you will be well.'

Bartimaeus blinked. Then he blinked again. He looked and there was someone smiling at him and that person was Jesus.

'I can see!' he yelled. 'I can see!'

Jesus just grinned and carried on walking, followed by lots and lots of people. And one of those people following him was Bartimaeus.

Thinking time...

Bartimaeus followed Jesus and found out as much as he could about him. Explore what it means to follow someone (think of examples from pop groups, footballers, friendship groups).

Why do we follow other people? Are they always good people to follow?

Christians believe Jesus is the very best person to follow.

Prayer...

Dear God,

Thank you that, like Bartimaeus, we have the choice to follow Jesus if we want to and find out more about him.

Amen.

Showing friendship to others

6

Jesus meets Zacchaeus

Children will...

- think about trees
- take part in the story of Zacchaeus (Luke 19:1–9)
- think about how they can show friendship to others

You'll need...

- pictures of trees
- container with money in
- plastic money
- dressing up clothes
- something safe for 'Zacchaeus' to stand on

Introduction...

Talk about different types of **trees**. What can the children do when the branches are low down? (*Climb them.)*

Story...

Jesus went to a place called Jericho. A man called Zacchaeus lived there. We know several things about Zacchaeus.

1 He lived in Jericho.
2 He collected taxes from people. Tax is money that people pay to the government for public services like hospitals and schools, or in Jesus' time, for the army. Tax collectors did not have many friends because they used to cheat.
(Ask a child to come to the front to act out Zacchaeus collecting taxes. Take more money than is needed. Discuss how the children feel about that.)
3 Zacchaeus was rich. How had he got rich?
4 He was small.

And then Jesus turned up. Everybody had heard about Jesus and the things he did, so people left what they were doing and went to see him. A huge crowd gathered round Jesus and Zacchaeus found himself pushed to the back. All he could see were people's heads and shoulders.

(Ask the children to act the story out.)

So, what did he do? He ran on ahead to where Jesus was going to walk and found a fig tree with low branches which he climbed. He could see now, and watched as Jesus came along the road.

(Discuss what part of Jesus' head he would have seen.)

And when Jesus got to the tree, he looked up and said to Zacchaeus, 'Hurry down, Zacchaeus, because I must come to your house today.'

(Discuss the reaction of the crowd to this statement and what part of Jesus' face Zacchaeus now saw.)

Well, Zacchaeus hurried down from the tree. He took Jesus to his house where they talked for a long time. The Bible doesn't tell us what they talked about, but we do know that at one point Zacchaeus stood up and said, 'Listen. I will give half my belongings to the poor, and if I have cheated anyone, I will pay back four times as much.'

(Ask the child who paid taxes at the beginning to return and be paid four times as much by Zacchaeus.)

Thinking time...

Jesus didn't mind that Zacchaeus was a cheat and did not have many friends. He treated everyone the same. Is that easy, or is it hard to like some people?
When Jesus was kind to Zacchaeus and became his friend, Zacchaeus changed.

Prayer...

Dear God,
It's lovely when you know other people want to be your friend. Help us to be good friends to everyone, just like Jesus was.
Amen.

Getting ready for Christmas

some background information about Jesus' birth

This assembly can be linked to Advent (four weeks before Christmas).

Children will...

- be introduced to the idea that Advent is a time of waiting
- consider some of the background to the Christmas story
- think about how they will get ready for Christmas

You'll need...

- Advent calendar or ring
- OHP with paper to cover up parts of acetate
- Bible, to show passage of time
- pictures on pages 32–34

Introduction...

Discuss **Advent calendars** or Advent rings and ask how (if they celebrate Christmas) the children and their families are getting ready for it. Introduce the concept of **waiting**.

For Christians Advent is a time of waiting, too.

Story...

1 A long time ago, right at the beginning of the Bible, people were living on the earth. Sometimes they were nice to each other but sometimes they weren't.
(Show Picture 1 on acetate – child kicking another child.)
What other things do people do to each other that are not very nice?

2 And when they wanted to be friends again, what did they have to say to each other?
(Show Picture 2 on acetate – saying sorry.)

3 Christians believe that God wanted, and still wants everyone to be his friend. But every time people did something that was wrong and didn't say sorry, they were showing him they didn't want to be his friend. So God decided to come to earth and live as a person and he was called... *(Jesus.)*
(Show Picture 3 on acetate – different stages of human growth.)

4 Now, before Jesus was born, people who could tell what was going to happen in the future, called prophets, said that God's special messenger was going to come to earth. One of the prophets was called Micah. He said that a town called Bethlehem would be very important.
(Show Picture 4 on acetate – prophet.)

5 Just before Jesus was born, the Roman army took over the country where Bethlehem is. They took over Israel and made everyone go to the place where they were born and pay them some money. So Mary, who was Jesus' mother, went with Joseph to Bethlehem.
(Show Picture 5 on acetate – Mary and Joseph.)

6 And while they were there, in Bethlehem, Mary had her baby. He was God's son, and he was called... Jesus.
(Show Picture 6 on acetate – baby Jesus.)
Advent is a time of getting ready, for waiting, for getting excited about Jesus being born.

How would Mary have got ready for her baby?
What do you think Christians do to get ready for Christmas?
(Pray, read the story in the Bible, go to church services, do something for other people, such as charity work.)

Thinking time...

What are you looking forward to most about this Christmas-time? Can you think of one thing you will be doing that might remind you about Jesus being born?

Prayer...

Dear God,
Christmas is a really exciting time of year. Help us to remember that it is when you came to earth as a baby.
Amen.

I’m Sorry

C.E.

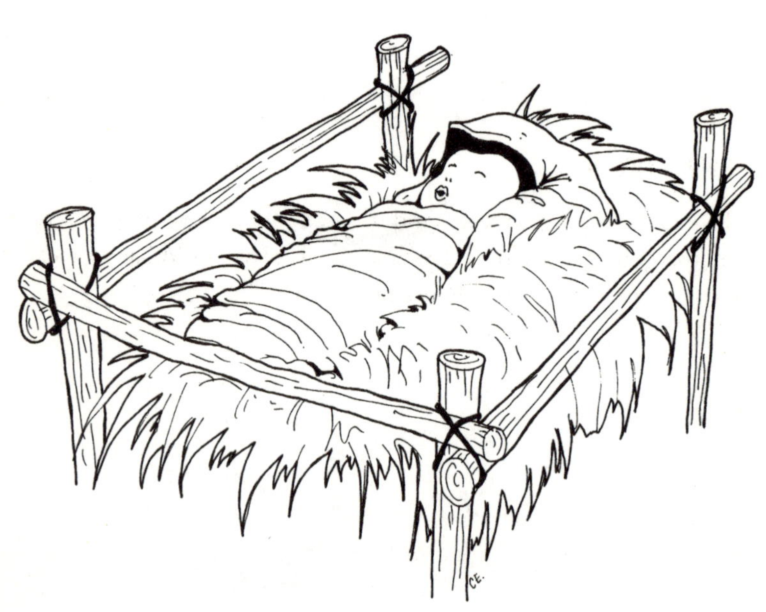
C.E.

Being lost and found

8

Jesus' parable about a lost coin

Children will...

- look at a lamp (or candle) and think about its uses
- hear the parable of the lost coin (Luke 15:8–10)
- draw parallels about what it feels like to be lost and found themselves

You'll need...

- a light source such as a lamp or candle
- 10 silver coins
- brush (for sweeping the floor)

Introduction...

Talk about **light sources** and discuss their uses. For example, camping, barbecues, birthday candles, decorations. What happens if there's a power cut or if there's no electricity?

Story...

Jesus told a story about a lamp.

There was a woman who had ten silver coins. That was a lot of money.

Now, one day she went to get the coins, and there were only nine. What do you think she did? *(Discuss the options...*

forgot about the coin, looked for it, asked someone to help her, got upset.

Ask a child to act out what the woman did.)

She went to where her lamp was and lit it because her house had lots of really dark corners. Then she used a brush and began sweeping her house right through, from top to bottom. And all the time she was looking for that one silver coin. It had to be somewhere.

If you look for something really carefully, what usually happens? *(You find it!)*

That's what happened in the story. At last she found the coin, and when she did, she was so excited that she called her friends and neighbours in.

'I'm so happy!' she said. 'I've found the coin that was lost!'

When he told that story, Jesus said something else. He said that God gets excited, just like the woman did when she found her silver coin. God gets excited every time a boy or girl or grown up talks to him.

Thinking time...

Have you ever been lost?
What did it feel like?
And then what did it feel like to be found?
Do you ever feel lost in the playground, maybe when you haven't got anyone to play with?
And then how do you feel when someone asks you to play with them?

Prayer...

Ask the children for suggestions of things to tell God about before you pray. The children might want to pray about looking out for 'lost' people, being loved and being part of the school community.

Dear God,
Thank you that we talk to you when we pray. Here are a few things we'd like to tell you about. *(Pause for the children to pray.)*
Amen.

Giving presents

Jesus is born

This assembly can be linked to Christmas preparations.

Children will...

- look inside a cracker
- make a time line of the key events in the Christmas story (Luke 2:1–20 and Matthew 2:1–12) and think what would go in a cracker to celebrate Jesus' birthday
- consider what they can give at Christmas time

You'll need...

- cracker
- paper and thick felt-tip pens (for drawing)
- large piece of paper to make shell of cracker with string to tie cracker up
- cymbal

Introduction...

Open a cracker and look at what is inside: joke, present, hat, 'crack'. Discuss when crackers are used and why.

Story...

We're going to make a cracker for Jesus' birthday party to help remind us of what happened at Christmas.

(Take suggestions from the children about what happens in the Christmas story. Draw each suggestion and ask different children to hold each drawing up. Then tell the story, putting the pictures in the correct place to make a time line.)

It was nearly time for Mary to have her baby.

'Time to go,' Joseph said.

They had a long journey ahead of them to Bethlehem. That was the village where Joseph had been born and they were going there to pay some money to the Romans. Lots of other people were going there too.

When they arrived there was nowhere for them to stay. They were so tired. At last, someone said there was a stable they could use.

'Thank you,' Joseph said.

He helped Mary get off the donkey she had been riding on and made a bed of straw so she could lie down. It wasn't long before there was a baby's cry. Jesus, the Son of God, had come in to the world, born in a stable.

Near Bethlehem, some shepherds were looking after their sheep when suddenly there was a great big flash of light and singing in the sky. The shepherds were really scared! Angels appeared, sent from God to tell them about Jesus being born.

'Let's go and find out about Jesus,' they said when the angels left them. So they did. They left their sheep and went down to Bethlehem and found Mary and Joseph and baby Jesus.

Mary and Joseph stayed in Bethlehem for a long time. As soon as there was room they moved out of the stable to a proper house and it was there that some wise men came to visit them with gifts of gold, frankincense and myrrh. The gold was to show that Jesus was a king.

(Draw a crown.

Add the motto, a letter to wish Jesus a happy birthday. Either ask the children to make one up or use this one: 'Dear Jesus, happy birthday. Thanks for coming. Love...' Put it with the crown and drawings of the Christmas story.

For the 'crack' make a loud bang with a cymbal, then sing

a Christmas song like the angels would have done.

Lastly, take the children's suggestions as to which presents they could give to Jesus. Draw them and wrap the drawings up in a larger sheet of paper to make the cracker.)

Thinking time...

The shepherds and the wise men brought presents for Jesus. We too can give presents. What can we give? To whom? Which charities have the children heard of this Christmas?
Christmas is a time for giving. Christians believe it's the time when God gave his son to the world.

Prayer...

Dear God,
We've been thinking about some of the people who went to the first Christmas party. They brought presents with them. Thank you that we can give presents as well.
Amen.

New year resolutions

some ideas from Jesus' teaching

This assembly could possibly be split in to two parts, breaking where the puppet is introduced.

Children will...

- talk about new year resolutions
- think about some of Jesus' teaching given in the 'Sermon on the Mount' (Matthew 5:4–9)
- consider how each idea is important to themselves

You'll need...

- 'resolutions' written out on large pieces of paper
- puppet

Introduction...

Talk about the beginning of the **new year** and how it is celebrated. Have the children, or anyone they know, made any **resolutions**? Resolutions are promises to start again. (Give an example.) What are your resolutions?
Have the children stuck to them?

Story...

Jesus said some things that would make good resolutions.

- Jesus said that it's OK **to get upset (mourn)**
  Why do we sometimes get upset?
  Who could you tell if you were really sad about something?
  What would you do if someone told you they were upset?
- Jesus said to **be humble**
  Being humble means putting other people before yourself. Can you think of an example of what this means?
  How do you feel when someone makes you feel important? Can you think of an example in the classroom when being humble would be a good thing?
- Jesus said to **be kind to other people**
  How can you be kind to other people?
- Jesus said to **think nice thoughts about other people**
  (Make a list of nice thoughts.)
- Jesus said to **work for peace**
  How can you do this? Is it always easy? Who can help?

POSSIBLE BREAK HERE (if you're not breaking, move to the point marked * * * at the top of page 45)

Thinking time...

Think about a time when you have been sad... or humble... or kind... or thought nice things... or wanted peace. What did it feel like? Are they good things to try and do this year?

Prayer...

Dear God,
Help us to try to do what is right, even when it's difficult.
Amen.

* * *

If you are extending this to two assemblies, recap the first part before introducing the puppet.

Let the puppet speak and act out the sentences below and discuss whether it's sticking to any of the resolutions.

- I'm really sad about my sister being ill.
- You two, stop arguing and shouting at each other.
- I'd love to be first in the dinner queue, but I'm going to let Ben go first.
- Do you want a sweet?
- Isn't she a nice person?
- I don't mind him playing the game. I'll watch for a while.
- I'll look after you.
- Do you want to play football with us?
- Let's see if she wants to come swimming with us after school.
- I don't like him. He's horrible.

Thinking time...

Think of an easy resolution to make and keep.

Now think of a harder one.

Why is it harder?

Possible extension work...

Can the children put the five 'resolutions' in order of difficulty to achieve... and explain their ordering?

There is also the possibility of discussing feelings of failure.

Prayer...

Dear God,

You said that anyone who tries to do what you want will be happy.

Help us to think about what we do and how it affects other people.

Thank you that if we do get it wrong, if we ask you, you will help us to do better.

Amen.

Presents that don't cost anything

11

Jesus is visited by the wise men

This assembly can be linked to the Christian festival of Epiphany (12 January).

Children will...

- see a time line of important events
- hear about wise men visiting Jesus when he was a baby (Matthew 2:1–12)
- think about gifts they can give to each other

You'll need...

- string, pegs, possibly a compass
- 'signposts': write out 'Jerusalem', 'The East' and 'Bethlehem' on card
- a star shape, or pictures of stars
- any information about stars you might want to include
- enlarged photocopy of camels and wise men on pages 51 and 52
- chair for Herod's throne

Introduction...

Look at pictures of **stars** or star shapes and talk about them. For example, the sun, which is a star, is 150 million kilometres away from planet earth and the next nearest star is millions of kilometres even further away. All stars are part of our galaxy.

Story...

People used to believe that when a new star appeared in the sky it was because a new king had been born.

Long ago, there were some wise men who used to look up at the stars.

'There's a new star,' they said one day. 'A king must have been born. Let's go and find out who he is and worship him.'

(Ask the children if they know what the word 'worship' means. Explain that it's to adore, to make a person or thing more important than yourself.)

So the three wise men set off on their journey. The Bible doesn't actually tell us they went on camels, but it's a pretty good guess that they did.

(Set up a piece of string across the front of the hall. Possibly work out east and west to get the direction correct. Attach the camels and wise men illustration from the photocopiable sheet on the east side of the string and move it across towards Jerusalem with Herod sitting on his throne in the middle of the string above a chair.

Ask the children where they would look for a baby king then choose a child to be Herod and sit him on the chair. Herod can have servants who check he is having a good day.)

And then came the wise men. The Bible doesn't actually tell us there were three, but there were three gifts so lots of people think there probably were three.

(Choose three children to be the wise men and approach Jerusalem/Herod from the east and knock on the palace door.)

'What do you want?' Herod asked.

'Where is the baby born to be king of the Jews?' the wise men asked. 'We saw his star when it came up in the east, and we have come to worship him.'

(Ask Herod if he is still having a nice day.

Oh, he's not.

Ask Herod why he's not happy. Herod knows nothing of any new king just been born. How dare these men tell him there is a new king! He's the only king.)

But Herod was worried. He asked for some clever people to come to him, and he asked them if they had any ideas about this new king.

'Well,' they said, 'in our holy book, it says that a leader will be born in Bethlehem.'

And Herod went, 'AAAAGH!!!!' because Bethlehem was just down the road from Jerusalem. Herod thought for a few minutes.

'Right,' he said. 'I have a cunning plan. Get those wise men over here.' *(Wise men go to Herod.)*

'Go and make a careful search for the child. When you find him, let me know, so that I too may go and worship him.'

Herod was not going to worship the new king. What do you think he planned to do to him?

So the wise men left and on their way they saw the same star moving across the night sky. They followed it to Bethlehem.

(Put 'Bethlehem' up on string further to the west.)

And when they arrived in Bethlehem they discovered that Mary and Joseph were not in the stable any more. They had moved somewhere else. And when the wise men found Jesus, they knelt down and worshipped him, giving him their gifts of gold, frankincense and myrrh.

Now, where had King Herod asked them to go next? *(Go to Herod.)*

Only they didn't, because in their dreams, God told them to go straight home.

Which is what they did.

(Take them off the string and walk them round Jerusalem, leaving Herod sitting on his throne.)

Thinking time...

The gifts the wise men gave to Jesus were really expensive.
What is the most expensive present you have ever had?
Christians believe that the most expensive present God ever gave was his son, Jesus. It didn't cost him any money, though.
We can give presents sometimes that don't cost any money. Can you think what we can give? (S*miles, love, being kind, friendly, helpful.)*

Prayer...

Dear God,
Thank you that you sent your son to earth as a tiny baby. If there is something we can give to other people that does not cost any money, please show us what it is.
Amen.

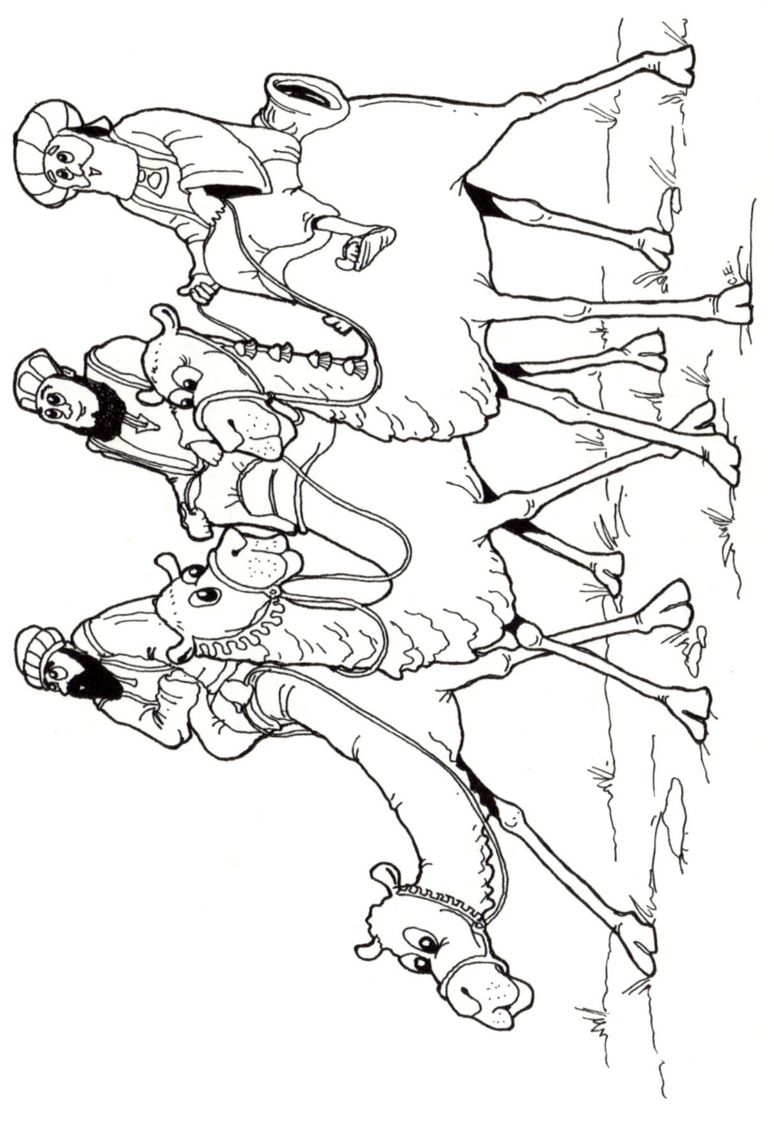

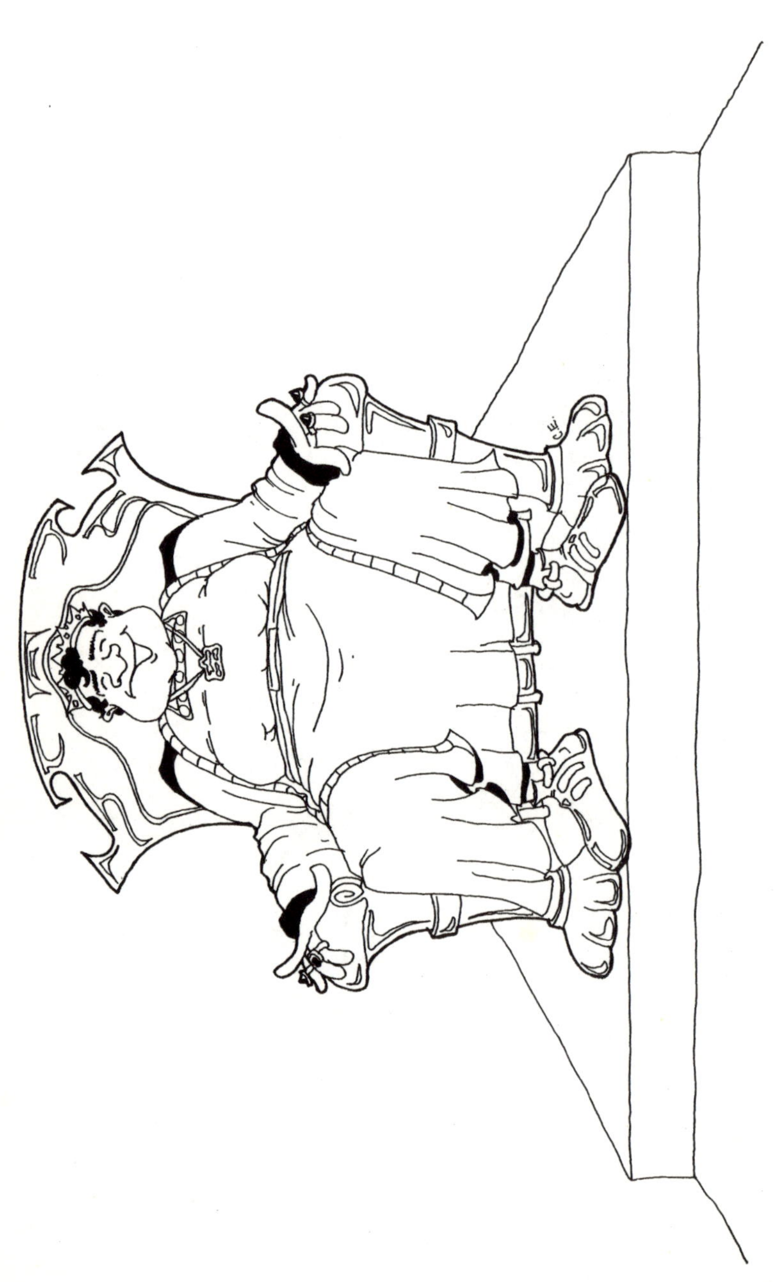

Forgiveness

Jesus heals a man lowered through a roof

Children will...

- think about how important a roof is
- take part in the story of Jesus healing a man whose friends took the roof off a house to reach Jesus (Mark 2:1–12)
- explore what the word 'forgiveness' means

You'll need...

- very large piece of paper (large enough to cut a hole in and slide a child through)
- scissors
- 4 strips of card joined by split pins to be used as a visual aid, folding the strip to make the flat roofed house, steps, bed and lowering the bed through the roof

Introduction...

Talk about **wet weather** and how important a **roof** is.

Story...

Jesus once went to a place called Capernaum and stayed at a house with a roof. At least, it had a roof before Jesus got there. It had steps up the side, and the people who owned the house often went up on to the roof. In Jesus' country people's houses had flat roofs.

What was the roof used for? *(Storing things, extra living space as it was a hot country.)*

Everyone soon found out Jesus was there and wanted to see him. So many people came to the house. They stared in at the windows, sat on each others' shoulders and stood on tip toes, just to hear what he was saying.

Now there was in Capernaum a man who couldn't walk. And he had four friends. Four rather brilliant friends. They decided to take their friend to see Jesus, so they put him on a stretcher and carried him to the house where Jesus was.

Now what was the problem? *(Too many people.)*

So what were they to do? *(Go up the steps to the roof!)*

(Hold the very large piece of paper flat for the roof and study it.)

It was a lovely roof, really useful if the sun was shining or the rain was falling or you wanted to climb the steps and sit on it. Now the people who were inside the house listening to Jesus telling them about God suddenly heard a scrabbling, scraping noise. Then bright sunlight suddenly burst through the roof and four pairs of hands were making the hole get bigger and bigger and bigger...

(Cut a hole in the paper roof.)

Until...

Right above Jesus' head was a hole big enough to lower the stretcher with the man on it.

(With help, feed child through hole in paper to demonstrate.)

Now what could Jesus have said to the man? *(Hello! What are you doing? Get up and walk! and healed him on the spot.)*

In fact, the Bible tells us that Jesus said, 'Your sins are forgiven.' What did Jesus mean by the word 'sins'? *(To do something wrong.)* What did Jesus mean by the word 'forgiven'? *(Forgotten.)*

Well, the crowd in the house looked at each other.

'You can't say that,' some of them thought. 'Only God forgives sins.'

'I can forgive sins,' Jesus said. Then he turned to the man and looked at him. I expect he smiled as well because he knew how excited the man was going to be in a few seconds' time.

'Get up!' he said. 'Pick up your bed, and go home!'

Now remember, the house was completely full and the man was up in the air. So what were the crowd going to have to do? *(Move to make space for him, breathe in!)*

You'd have got very squashed if you were at the edge of the room.

And the man did as Jesus said. He got up and left. I expect his friends left too, before the owner of the house got hold of them. The Bible doesn't say, but I hope it didn't rain before the roof was repaired.

Thinking time...

Jesus said he could forgive. What did the word 'forgive' mean?
Have you ever forgiven someone?
Has anyone ever forgiven you?
Is forgiving people easy or hard?
God says he will always forgive us and be our friend, whatever we have done.

Prayer...

Dear God,
Forgiving and forgetting can be really difficult. Thank you that you forgive us if we are really sorry about doing something we shouldn't have done. Help us to learn how to forgive and forget as well.
Amen.

Showing love

13

sending a special card to God

This assembly can be linked to Valentine's Day (14 February).

Children will...

- look at Valentine cards and discuss why they are given
- think about love in the context of friendship (Luke 10:38), families (Matthew 13:55–56), people we meet (Luke 8:41–48), and unconditional love (Luke 17:12–19)
- make a special card to send to God
- think about how people show other people they love them

You'll need...

- OHP with the 4 rhymes below on acetate
- 4 rhymes cut out ready to stick in the card
- paper, pens, glue stick

Introduction...

Look at some **Valentine cards** and introduce the idea of different types of **love** – to friends, families, people we meet, and when nothing is given back in return.

Story...

We're going to send God a special (Valentine) card. *(Show the large sheet of folded paper and put the first poem on the OHP.)*

My hair needs a comb, I've got dirty knees

But all of my friends, look after them please.

(Ask questions to develop the idea of friendship love. For example… how do we love our friends? Do they mind what we look like? Do we have to think about being nice to them? Do we ever say sorry to them?)

Jesus had friends. He had 12 special friends as well as people like Mary and Martha who lived in a village called Bethany. He used to call in and see them sometimes. He knew how important friends were.

(Ask some children to stick the rhyme in the card and ask different groups of friends to come together and sign the card.)

(Move on to the second rhyme.)

Bananas are yellow, mushrooms are white
Thanks for my family, even when we fight.

(Ask questions to develop the idea of love within families. For example:

Who knows more about you, your friends or your family? What do you do as a family that is special? Who is the most important person in your family? What happens when you get fed up with each other? If you've had a fight or an argument, how do you get back to being friends again?)

Jesus was in a family, too. His earthly father, Joseph, was a carpenter. Mary was his mother and we know he had brothers called James, Joseph, Simon and Judas. He had some sisters as well. So he knows what it's like living in a family.

(Ask if any brothers/sisters/cousins in school would like to stick the rhyme in the card and then sign it.)

(Move on to the third rhyme.)

Roses are red, violets are blue
Unhappy people, we'll look after you too.

(Ask questions to develop the idea of helping people we don't know. For example: can anyone think of someone we help who we don't know? How can we show people we don't know that we care about them? For example, buying poppies, giving to charities and appeals. What local projects are there?)

Jesus cared about everyone. He had a crowd all round him once and there was an old lady who was ill. She struggled to the front of the crowd.

'If I just touch his clothes I'll get well,' she said.

And that was exactly what happened. She touched Jesus' clothes and was healed.

And because Jesus loves and cares about everyone, he knows all about people who are hurting inside and hurts with them. It must make him happy when other people look after them as well.

(Ask some children who have given to a charity/bought a poppy to stick in the rhyme and sign the card.)

(Move on to the fourth rhyme.)

My gums they are pink, my teacher's tall
Real love is giving and getting nothing back at all.

We've thought about friends, families and those people we don't know. What about when you're nice to someone and they're nasty back? What do you do then?

Even though Jesus healed and helped people, some of them didn't like him. He still carried on loving them. That's a very special sort of love. That's bigger and stronger than Valentine cards with their little messages, bigger even than the love we have for friends and families. It didn't make any difference to Jesus what people said or did, he still went on loving them.

(Ask some children to stick the last rhyme in the card.)

Thinking time...

What does it feel like to know you've got lots of friends?
Do you know anyone who hasn't got many friends?
Can you think of something you could do to help them? Maybe you will need to show some real love.

Prayer...

Dear God,
Thank you that you know what it's like to have friends. You also know what it's like to have people being nasty to you and carry on loving them. Help us to love our friends, our families, those people we don't know well and those we find hard to like.
Amen.

Loving everyone

14

Jesus' story about the Good Samaritan

Children will...

- think about different ways to represent movements and sounds
- use these in the story of the Good Samaritan (Luke 10:30–37)
- reflect on how the story shows how to love other people

You'll need...

- the story as written below

Introduction...

Ask the children to suggest ways of representing the following things...

- flies (bzzzzz)
- a person/people who didn't care (shrug of the shoulders)
- a kind person (friendly smile)
- robbers (clenched fist and shout)
- an innkeeper (say 'Can I help you?')
- a man (stand up and bow)

Either have 6 children at the front doing the sounds and actions or else divide all the children into 6 groups.

Story...

Read the story and every time the appropriate word is read the children respond with the correct action or sound.

There was once a **man** who was going from Jerusalem to Jericho.

Now the road he travelled on had rocks on either side. High, jagged rocks, perfect for **robbers** to hide behind. It was a good place for **flies** as well. They liked the shade behind the rocks where the **robbers** hid.

Well, as the **man** walked down the road, **robbers** watched him and jumped out from behind the rocks. He tried to run away, but they beat him up, then left him lying on the road. The only things that saw it all were the **flies** who buzzed around and felt sorry for the poor **man**.

He lay there for a long time. The sun was hot and no one was there apart from the **flies** who eventually gave up buzzing round him and went back to the shade behind the rocks.

After a while, the **man** heard some footsteps. Someone's coming to help me, he thought. It was a priest. Now priests were important people who worked in the temple. You would expect them to do the right thing which would be... *(To go and help the man.)*

But when the priest saw the **man**, he crossed over and walked by on the other side of the road because he was a **person who didn't care**. No, all he thought about was himself and a **person who doesn't care** doesn't bother with other people.

So the **man** who had been attacked by the **robbers** lay in the hot sun until... someone else came along. This time it was a levite. Levites helped the priests in the temple. Not quite as important as the priests, but you would expect them to do the right thing.

The **flies** spotted the levite and flew out to see what he would do. They watched him spot the **man** and have a good look at him lying there in the road. But then the **flies** realised that the levite was a **person who didn't care** because he just ignored him and walked on.

Don't worry if you're a **kind person**, you're about to

become very busy because the next person who came along that road came from a place called Samaria. It was really sad because the priests and the levites and lots of other really important people who lived in Jerusalem had decided they didn't like people who lived in Samaria. They were nasty to them.

In Jesus' story the person from Samaria came up to the **man** that the **robbers** had left for dead, and when he saw him, he felt really sad because he was a **kind person**. And being a **kind person**, unlike the **people who didn't care**, or the **flies** who just buzzed round and made a lot of noise, he went over to him, poured oil and wine on his wounds and put bandages on them.

Then, being a **kind person**, he put the **man** on his own animal, which was probably a donkey, swatted the **flies**, made sure there weren't any more **robbers** around and took him to an inn. What a **kind person** he was. He certainly wasn't **someone who doesn't care**.

But that's not all, for he took out two silver coins and gave them to the **innkeeper**.

'Take care of him,' he told the **innkeeper**, 'and when I come back this way I will pay you whatever else you spend on him.'

The **innkeeper** said he would do that. The **innkeeper** must have thought what a very **kind person** the Samaritan was, not like the **robbers** or the **people who didn't care** or even the **flies** who went back to hiding in the shade of the rocks.

No, the **kind person**, the Samaritan, the one the priest and the levite and lots of others didn't like much, was the one who did the right thing.

Thinking time...

This wording avoids the key words from the story.
Who did the first important person in the story care about most? Remember he crossed the road to avoid the problem.

And the second person?
What about the Samaritan? Remember, the important people did not like him at all. When Jesus was telling the story most people would have expected him to make the Samaritan the one to do the wrong thing. But Jesus didn't do that. It was the Samaritan who did the right thing. He got off his donkey, crossed over the road, and then cared for the person lying in the road.
How can you help other people? Sometimes it is easy, but if you help someone who isn't really a friend, then you are being just like the Good Samaritan.

Prayer...

Dear God,
It's not always easy to be like the Good Samaritan. Please help us to think about other people all the time.
Amen.

Reaping what you sow 15

Jesus' story about the sower

Children will...

- discuss where seeds are planted and what they need to grow healthily
- take part in the parable of the sower from Matthew 13:1–9
- think about how they will grow as people

You'll need...

- bag (for seeds)
- packet of seeds

Introduction...

Show the children a packet of **seeds** or young plants and discuss conditions seeds need to **grow**. (*No birds, good soil without rocks, soil deep enough for roots to grow, not too much sun, not choked by other plants, water.)*
Talk about methods of farming before useful machines were invented.

Story...

Ask the children to join in with the actions for each part of the story.

Jesus told a parable about a farmer who sowed some seed. All he had was a large bag full of seed and he walked up and down the field throwing the seed over the soil.

Some of the seed landed on the path. *(Make hands flat to represent the path.)*

What's going to happen to the seed? *(Birds eat it.)*

That's exactly what happened. The birds flew down and had their dinner and the seed was no more. *(Children blow seed away.)*

Some of the seed fell on to rocks. *(Make rocks with hands.)*

What's going to happen to the seed now? *(Not enough soil.)*

Even though there wasn't much soil on the rocks the seeds did their best and started to grow... until the sun beat down and fried the little plants.

The farmer wasn't doing very well, was he? His seed had fallen on the path and rocks. And then some of it ended up by some thorn bushes. *(Make thorn bushes with fingers.)*

Nasty things, thorn bushes. They've got long spikes and their roots go really deep, taking out all the water they can find. So what happens to any seeds that fall near them? *(They choke and die.)*

And the seed near to the thorn bushes died, along with all the other seeds. So why does he do it? Why doesn't the farmer just go home and put his feet up?

The farmer doesn't give up because some of the seed fell on good soil. The seed began to grow roots and soon popped out of the ground. Then it got bigger and bigger and grew and grew and before long, fine stalks of corn waved as the wind blew across the field.

Thinking time...

Jesus said that our minds are like the soil. We hear all sorts of things. Ask for volunteers who will act out/say which sort of soil is about to be illustrated.

1 Hitesh is new to our school. You are nice to him at first then ignore him. Are you like the path, the rocks, the thorns or the good soil? *Rocks, because you start out well but don't continue.*
2 Your teacher tells you that 3 + 4 = 7 and you remember it. Are you like the path, the rocks, the thorns or the good soil? *Good soil, because you remember the good thing you have been told.*
3 Sarah is your friend, but she bosses you around and tells you what to do all the time. Is she like the path, the rocks, the thorns or the good soil? *Thorns, because it gets harder and harder to be friends.*
4 Jermaine is upset. You try to cheer him up, but he ignores you. Is he like the path, the rocks, the thorns or the good soil? *Path, because you do something good but it has no chance to grow.*
5 You are doing a job for your teacher. You start doing it but don't finish. Are you like the path, the rocks, the thorns or the good soil? *Rocks, because you start out well but don't continue.*
6 Someone hits you in the playground. You walk away because you've been told that thumping them back is not the thing to do. Are you like the path, the rocks, the thorns or the good soil? *Good soil, because you do something good, even though it's difficult.*

Which soil is the best?
Why?
Jesus said that if we do what he told us to do we are like the good soil.
Can you think of things he said to do? *(Love each other, be kind, trust him, look after each other.)*

Prayer...

Dear God,
You are like the farmer, planting ideas and thoughts. We are sorry when we are like the path and the rocks and the thorns and don't do the things you want us to do. We want to be good soil where lots of good things can grow.
Amen.

Looking after each other (16)

Jesus' story about the lost sheep

Children will...

- think about newborn lambs and how they need looking after
- take part in the story of the lost sheep in Luke 15:4–7
- consider who is there to look after them if they need help

You'll need...

- a representation of a lamb – eg picture, cuddly toy
- shepherd's crook/walking stick

Introduction...

Talk about newborn lambs, especially how they quickly become independent and can survive on their own; the bleating noise they make to talk to their mothers who look after them; and the shepherd's role in looking after them.

Story...

Jesus told a story about a lamb and a shepherd. The shepherd had a hundred sheep and he looked after them very carefully. At night, he brought them in from the field and put them in the sheepfold which had a little gate. As each sheep came through the gate, he would check to make sure the sheep was all right.

And every morning he would count the sheep to make sure none of them had got away during the night.

(Count on from 94 to 100.) All there, safe and sound.

Now one night the shepherd was counting his sheep. *(Count on from 94 to 99.)*

How many should there have been?

One was lost.

Now, what's the shepherd going to do? *(Leave it, ask someone else to go and look for it, go himself.)*

This shepherd was a good shepherd and he was very worried about the little lamb that was lost. One of his special, precious little lambs was out in the hills where something terrible might happen to it. There was only one thing to do. The shepherd must go and find it, even if it meant going to somewhere dangerous. So he made sure the other sheep were all right, picked up his shepherd's crook and headed off.

(Walk round or through the children, looking. Ask them to pretend to be trees, tall grass swaying in the wind, thick bushes, caves, rocks, prowling animals, different weather conditions, thorn bushes, cliffs.)

And then he heard a little bleating sound. There was the little lamb! He was so frightened. The shepherd gently picked up the little lamb, put it on his shoulders and carried it back home. It didn't matter that the lamb had been silly and run away from the sheep fold. It didn't matter that the shepherd had had to go a long way to bring him home again. The most important thing was that the little lamb was safe.

Thinking time...

The shepherd really looked after all his sheep, even when they ran away.

Who cares and looks after you? How do you know they care and look after you?

Do you ever say 'thank you' to them?

Prayer...

Dear God,
Thank you that you are like the good shepherd in the story. You love and care for each one of us, even when we do things we shouldn't. Lots of other people look after us as well. Thank you for them.
Amen.

Doing the right thing

Jesus is tempted to do the wrong thing

This assembly can be linked to the beginning of Lent, especially Shrove Tuesday.

Children will...

- talk about pancakes and why they are made today
- hear how Jesus was tempted (Matthew 4:1–11)
- think about how they can do the 'right' thing

You'll need...

- pictures of desolate/desert places
- ingredients for making pancakes

Introduction...

Pancake day is also called **Shrove Tuesday**. In the Christian calendar, it marks the day before Ash Wednesday, which is the beginning of **Lent**. Lent begins 40 days before Easter and is seen as a time of preparation for the most important event in the Christian faith: Jesus rising from the dead. During Lent, some people give up chocolate or don't watch television or go without eating. The idea is that they try to spend more time praying instead of doing these other things.

On Shrove Tuesday, pancakes were made to use up rich food like cooking fat, eggs, butter, flour and milk to make way for a different diet.

Story...

Lent is a time of 'getting ready' for Easter. The forty days of Lent is the same amount of time Jesus spent in the desert before he started doing miracles and telling stories about God. Forty days. That is a very long time.

Until Jesus was thirty he lived in Nazareth with his family. Joseph, his earthly father, was the village carpenter and Jesus would have learned how to be a carpenter as well. But when he was thirty, Jesus knew he had to do something else. He was to leave his home and start telling people about God, his heavenly father. But before he started this new work, he went in to the desert to pray.

Can you tell me what the desert is like?

Jesus went to the desert to be alone. He spent time praying, thinking and preparing for what he was about to do. He would have had all sorts of thoughts. He could make stones turn in to bread if he wanted to. He could have anything he liked. He could have crowds following and cheering everywhere he went, or have the biggest, strongest donkey to ride on. Anything.

What might you have wanted if you had been Jesus?

But Jesus said, 'no.' He was on earth to tell people about God.

Jesus was tempted. That means he could have done something but knew it was not the right thing to do, so he did not do it.

Thinking time...

If I had promised to see a friend who was not very well and then found out there was a good film on at the cinema, what might I be tempted to do?

Or if I was doing a spelling test and my friend didn't cover her answers up. What might I be tempted to do?

Ask the children to suggest other times they might be tempted to do the wrong thing.

Prayer...

Dear God,
It's often hard to do the right thing all the time. You know that because you lived on earth and were tempted to do the wrong thing. Thank you that you know how difficult it is sometimes.
Amen.

Betrayal

Jesus is betrayed

This assembly tackles concepts for older KS1 children and can be linked to Lent/Easter.

Children will...

- be introduced to the idea of hats representing different feelings and actions
- hear how Judas decided to betray Jesus (Mark 14:10,11)
- consider how friendships are affected by unkindness or betrayal

You'll need...

- selection of hats such as sun hat, woolly hat, flat cap, straw hat, baseball cap

Introduction...

Introduce the hats and the moods they could represent. For example:

wearing a sun hat could make you feel happy;
a woolly hat pulled down, angry;
a flat cap, worried;
a sports cap, excited;
a dull, boring hat, jealous because you want a hat like everyone else has;
a straw hat, excited.

Ask some children to put on one of the hats and say how they feel and what they might now do.

Story...

Some people followed Jesus and were happy listening to him and doing what he said.

(Ask a child to choose one of the hats.)

But not everyone liked Jesus. Some people were very jealous of him.

(Ask a child to choose a hat to represent jealousy.)

A bit like if someone does something really well and you wish you could do it like they do. That could make you a bit jealous.

Every time Jesus went somewhere, a crowd turned out to see him and hear what he had to say. That made some people very angry.

(Ask a child to choose a hat to represent anger.)

If your friend supported the same football team as you and then started supporting a different team, you might get a bit angry and wonder why they had changed.

One of Jesus' twelve special friends was like that. His name was Judas Iscariot. He worked with Jesus and saw everything he did. And then he decided to do something.

(Read Mark 14:10,11.)

Judas went off to the chief priests to tell them where Jesus was. They were pleased to hear what he had to say, and promised to give him some money. So Judas started looking for a good chance to hand Jesus over to them.

(Discuss which hat would be worn by Judas as he went to the chief priests.)

Judas was going to give Jesus to the people who didn't like him. Judas knew that they would hurt his friend. Judas was given thirty silver coins for handing Jesus over to them.

It's a bit like if you told a secret to a friend you trusted and asked them not to tell anyone else, then they went and told everyone. What would it feel like?

Thinking time...

Jesus was let down by Judas. Think of a time when you've been let down by someone. Maybe they promised to do something with you and never turned up. What did it feel like?
Have you ever let someone down?

Prayer...

Dear God,
You know what it is like to have a friend who lets you down because it happened to you. Help me not to hurt other people and not let them down.
Amen.

Being special 19

Jesus has a last meal with his friends

This assembly can be linked to Easter.

Children will...

- think about how water is used to wash things
- take part in the story of Jesus washing his disciples' feet (John 13:4–8)
- think of ways to show others that they are important and special

You'll need...

- a large bowl of water
- towel
- sandal

Introduction...

Discuss what **water** is used for. Jesus used water to show his friends how important and special they were to him.

Story...

When Jesus was alive there weren't any proper roads and pavements like we have today. There were dirt tracks. Most people wore open-toed sandals, or walked in bare feet. Their feet got very dusty.

People who were rich had servants who did all the work for them. What sort of things do you think they did? *(Wash up, cook, washing, fetch water from well, clean, tidy, wash feet.)*

So when you arrived at a rich person's house the servant would...

(Ask some children to come to the front and have their feet washed. Alternatively, this can just be acted out.)

('Interview' both parties and ask what it is like to do the washing and to have your feet washed.)

Just before the first Easter, Jesus and his friends went to Jerusalem. They were going to have a meal together. They all went in to the room and sat down.

Then Jesus rose from the table, took off his outer garment (that would be like his coat) and tied a towel round his waist. He poured some water in to a large bowl and began to wash his friends' feet and dry them with the towel.

What do you think Jesus' friends felt like? This job was usually done by a servant and Jesus was not a servant. He was the Son of God.

Jesus came to Simon Peter.

Do you remember who Simon Peter was? *(Fisherman, brother of Andrew, often said things that other people were thinking but weren't brave enough to say.)*

'Are you going to wash my feet?' Simon Peter asked. Jesus nodded.

'Never will you wash my feet! You are the Lord, the Son of God. You're not going to do it.'

Jesus probably gave him one of those looks that said, 'Oh yes I am!' before saying, 'If I don't wash your feet, you will no longer be one of my special friends.'

Jesus knew that real friends do things for each other that aren't always very nice to do. Your mums might sometimes think 'I'm so tired I don't really want to get a meal ready tonight'. But they still do it. Why?

Jesus washed his friends' feet that day because he wanted to show them how important each one of them was, and how special they were to him. He loved them enough to wash their feet and become like a servant to them.

Thinking time...

How can you show your friends how special and important they are to you?
How do other people show you how important and special you are to them?

Prayer...

Dear God,
Jesus showed his friends how important and special they were to him by washing their feet. Help us to find ways to show our friends how special they are to us.
Amen.

The Easter story

Jesus comes back to life

This assembly can be linked to Easter.

Children will...

- think about Easter eggs and Easter celebrations
- hear what Christians believe happened on the first Easter (Luke 23:26–56 and John 20:1–18)
- reflect on what happened

You'll need...

- the story as written below

Introduction...

Talk about **Easter eggs,** what's inside them and why we have them. Easter eggs are a sign of **new life,** just like when a chick hatches out of an egg. Christians believe Jesus came back to life after he was killed.

Story...

Jesus had been in Jerusalem for several days and was with his special friends, his disciples. The soldiers came for him very late at night when not many people were around. All Jesus' friends ran away and left him on his own. He was taken to see a very important person called Pilate. Pilate blamed Jesus for causing a lot of trouble even though he hadn't done anything wrong. He then said Jesus should die.

The soldiers led Jesus away. They made him carry a huge cross made out of wood over his shoulders. Jesus kept falling over because the cross was so heavy and he was so tired.

The soldiers saw a man called Simon. They grabbed hold of him and made him carry Jesus' cross. Two other men, who were robbers, were there as well, carrying their wooden crosses. Finally, they reached a hill outside the city. They had to lie down on the wood, and nails were hammered through their hands and feet so they could be hung up on the crosses.

The soldiers laughed at Jesus. He could have come down off the cross if he had wanted to, but he chose not to.

At about twelve o'clock in the middle of the day darkness spread right over the land. It went completely black, as if it was night-time, and stayed like that for three hours.

Then Jesus cried out in a loud voice.

'Father,' he said, 'in your hands I place my spirit!'

And then he died.

Later on a man called Joseph went to Pilate and asked him if he could have Jesus' body. Joseph took the body down, wrapped it in a linen sheet and placed it in a tomb. A tomb is a hole dug out of a rock where bodies are put. Then a large stone was rolled across the entrance to the tomb so that no one could get in or out.

All that happened on a Friday. It's now known as Good Friday. Very early on Sunday morning, Jesus' friend, Mary, went to the tomb. She had the biggest shock of her life because the stone that had covered the entrance to the tomb had gone!

Mary thought someone had stolen Jesus' body and began to cry. After a while she saw someone else in the garden with her.

'If you took him away,' she said, 'tell me where you have put him.'

'Mary!' the man said.

Mary gasped. She knew that voice. It was Jesus. He had died, but he had come back to life again.

Thinking time...

Christians believe that Jesus died.

Christians also believe Jesus came back to life again. Only someone who was God could do that.

Think of one word that will remind you of what Christians believe happened at Easter. See if you can remember that as you eat any Easter eggs this year.

Prayer...

Dear God,

Thank you for Easter eggs, but thank you even more that you love us enough to let your son be born as a baby and live on this earth. Thank you that he died and then came back to life again.

Amen.

Making up

Jesus and his friends have breakfast together

This assembly can be linked to the time after Easter.

Children will...

- think about special meals
- take part in the account of Jesus having breakfast with his friends (John 21:1–15)
- think about how to make up with other people when they fall out

You'll need...

- bread and fish
- cards with disciples' names on – Simon Peter, Thomas, Nathanael, James, John

Introduction...

Talk about **special meals** the children have been to, who was there, what made it special, what they wore.

Story...

Jesus took part in a very special meal. It was at breakfast time, after he had died and come back to life again.

Some of his friends were fishing in the lake. Well, at least, they were trying to fish. They had been out all night and not a single fish had come anywhere near their boat. They had caught absolutely nothing.

There was Simon Peter, Thomas, Nathanael, James and John.

(Ask children to come to the front, give them name cards to hold up and ask them to act out the story.)

As the sun was rising, Jesus stood on the beach at the edge of the lake. His friends saw him but did not realise it was Jesus.

'Haven't you caught anything?' he called out.

'Not a thing,' they answered.

'Throw your net out on the right hand side of the boat, and you will catch some fish,' he shouted.

So they did. Then the problem began! Loads of fish swam into the nets. There were so many fish they couldn't pull their nets over the sides of the boat.

Then Simon Peter suddenly realised who was standing on the side of the lake.

'It is the Lord!' he shouted and jumped into the water. The Bible tells us that the boat was only about 100 metres from the shore, so it wasn't too far for him to swim.

Why do you think Simon Peter jumped overboard?

Now just before Jesus had died, Simon Peter had done something that wasn't very nice. Jesus was standing with the soldiers all around him and everyone was talking about him. Someone asked Simon Peter if he knew Jesus. Simon Peter pretended he didn't, even though he was one of Jesus' closest friends.

It would be a bit like me saying I didn't know _____ just because they were in trouble.

Well, as Simon Peter was swimming towards Jesus, the other friends brought the boat to the shore. There were 153 fish in their nets and Jesus had built a fire like a barbecue. He had some bread with him as well.

After they had eaten, Jesus said to Simon Peter, 'Do you love me?'

Now remember, Simon Peter had let Jesus down earlier, and if you let someone down, what do you have to do? *(Say sorry.)*

Jesus was giving Simon Peter a chance to say sorry. Simon Peter must have felt so glad to know Jesus wanted to be his friend again.

Thinking time...

If we fall out with our friends, we need to say sorry as well. Jesus and Simon Peter had a meal together.
Can you think of a time when you fell out with someone?
What did it feel like inside?
What did it feel like when you became friends again?
Which was the nicer feeling?

Prayer...

Dear God,
Simon Peter knew he was your special friend. You can be our special friend too. Thank you for that. Thank you for all our other friends as well.
Amen.

Making the world a happier place

22

Jesus' suggestion we should be like salt

This outline can be combined with 23 if a longer assembly is required.

Children will...

- think about how important salt is
- hear how Jesus described his followers as salt in Matthew 5:13–16
- consider how they can make the world a happier place

You'll need...

- food with salt in, including crisps with and without salt (dipping chips are often unsalted)
- photocopied script

Introduction...

Talk about how **salt** can make food taste better, how our bodies need salt (though not too much) and how salt helps food stay fresh, especially when there is no refrigeration (as when Jesus was alive).

Story...

Some foods taste better if a little salt is added.
(Ask for two volunteers to sample salted and unsalted crisps. Which do they prefer? Most people will say the former. A little salt brings out the taste in food.)

Our bodies need the right amount of salt.
(Ask a child to read the script below, photocopied if necessary.)

Me and my best friend go everywhere together. It's great to have a best friend because you've always got someone to talk to.

We talk about everything. Most of the time it's great but sometimes I want to be on my own. My best friend keeps wanting me to do things with him/her. That's when we fall out, but we usually make up again.

(Discuss the benefits of close friendship and the importance of giving each other space. With salt, we need to have the right amount to make food taste good. Parallel this with friendship.)

Salt makes food last longer.
(Ask two more children to come to the front. Imagine one of them is about to move away and go to another school. How can they keep being friends? For example, by writing, phoning, sending email, visiting.)

That is like putting salt on their friendship, because these things will help the friendship to last longer.

(Resume the three points – salt makes things taste better, you need the right amount, and makes food last longer. Recap the three friendship analogies.)

Thinking time...

Salt is important to us but we need just the right amount.
Can the children think of things they can do to be like salt and make the world a happier place?

Prayer...

Dear God,
Please help us become like salt in your world.
Amen.

Making the world a brighter place

23

Jesus' suggestion we should be like light

This outline can be combined with 22 if a longer assembly is required.

Children will...

- think about how important light is
- hear how Jesus described his followers as light in Matthew 5:13–16
- consider how they can make the world a happier place

You'll need...

- a light source/different light sources, eg a torch
- a box with a lid, containing a picture (of anything) inside and a pin hole in the side
- pictures, if available, of where lights are used

Introduction...

Without offering any light source, ask a child to say what the picture inside the box is. Then offer a light source and get an improved description because the child can see the picture more clearly.

Story...

Jesus said we were to be like a light. *(Pick up the torch and shine it in to the box again.)* A light helps us see things better, but what happens if the light is so bright it dazzles? *(We can't look – it's too bright.)*

What happens if the light is too dim? *(We can't see properly.)*

(Ask the children for ideas they have about where light is important. For example, lighthouses, traffic lights, electric lights when it's dark, guiding lights at the cinema, fire/beacons, in mines, tunnels, car headlights.

Recap the point that light shows more detail, but it needs to be bright enough without dazzling.)

Thinking time...

Ask the children to suggest ways they can be like light in the world to make it a happier, brighter place.
How can they be like light when they are... at home, at school, in the playground, with someone they don't like very much?

Prayer...

Here is a verse from the Bible.
'You are like salt. If salt loses its saltiness, there is no way to make it salty again. You are like light and your light must shine.'
Dear God,
Help us to be like salt and light.
Amen.

Being forgiven

Jesus' story about the lost son

This assembly is particularly appropriate if it's been raining.

Children will...

- think about the rain and look at some umbrellas
- hear the story of the lost son (Luke 15:11–32)
- think about how the father in the story forgave his son

You'll need...

- an umbrella
- words for the child playing the son to say enlarged and photocopied

Introduction...

Look at how **umbrellas** are made, and discuss when and how they are used.
Jesus told a story about a son who lived with his dad and his brother on a farm. Life was safe for the son, like being under an umbrella with your mum or dad when it is raining.

Story...

Ask children to come and act out the story with an umbrella as it is told.

One day, the son, who was safe at home with his dad *(hold umbrella over son and father)* decided he was going to find out what life was like in the big town a long way away. He knew his dad was rich and would be giving him some of his money later on, so he went to his dad and said...

'Dad, give me my share of the property NOW!'

No please. No thank you. Just the son telling his dad he wanted loads and loads of money.

Now, the father had a choice. He could let his son go, or he could make him stay at home when he really didn't want to be there. In the end he let him go.

So the son packed his bags, took his umbrella and set off to the big town a long way away.

And when he arrived in the big town he might have gone to the races. His umbrella would have been very useful for sitting on.

(Collapse umbrella and sit on handle.)

He probably lost lots of money there, but that didn't matter. He still had loads and loads more to spend.

He probably bought lots of new clothes.

(Hold umbrella to cover the boy's body while he mimes getting changed.)

'Do you like my new outfit? Only the best for me!'

There again, he might have used his umbrella to pull some of his mates out of the river when they fell in.

(Collapse umbrella and mime holding it out to friend in river.)

'There you are. Good thing I was around. Better come back with me. Here, lean on my umbrella. That'll help.'

Or played snooker...

(Use umbrella as cue.)

His house, well, I expect it was like a palace with bright lights, entertainment, servants... you name it, he had it.

(Put umbrella up and swirl it round.)

'What do you think of my house then? Good, eh?'

And as for the food the cook dished up… well, that had to be seen to be believed!

(Put umbrella with handle on floor to make a table.)

'Anything you want. I'll get it for you.'

And then one day, his money ran out. It didn't run out of the door or anything like that. There was simply none left. Nothing. He had no friends left, either. The whole lot left him and, to make matters worse, there wasn't much food around, either.

He ended up looking after a load of pigs. He sat all day watching pigs snort and roll in the mud and cough and trot and waddle.

(Hold umbrella open and upside down to make pigs' trough.)

He could well have taken some of the pigs' food home with him to eat, carrying it in his umbrella of course.

This was the boy who had once had everything and look at him now.

Well, after a while, he thought to himself,

'All my father's workers have more than they can eat, and here am I about to starve. I will get up and go to my father and say, "Father I have sinned against God and against you. Don't call me your son, treat me as one of your servants."'

That was brave of him. He was going back to his father to see if he could come home, not as his father's son, but as a servant.

A servant. Can you imagine it? This boy's been used to having everything done for him. But not any more.

So he set off, taking his umbrella with him. He likes his umbrella. But not as much as his father liked him because, do you know, his father was looking out for him! Staring down the road to see if today would be the day his son would come back to him.

And today was the day he had been waiting for!

'Whahay, he's here!' the father shouted. Or something like that, we don't know for sure. He raced down the road to meet his son.

'But I've done wrong,' the boy said. 'Treat me like a servant from now on.'

'No!' the father said. 'You've come home. Let's have a party and celebrate. I thought you were dead, but you're alive. I thought you were lost, but you're found.'

And that was what they did. And the father and the son stood together beneath the umbrella once more.

Thinking time...

The father was waiting, wanting his son to come home again because he loved him so much. He was happy to forgive and forget everything the son had done. *(Explore the meaning of forgiveness.)*
God is like that. It doesn't matter what we've done wrong, he will always forgive us if we ask him.
When have you forgiven someone? Was it easy? Was it the right thing to do?

Prayer...

Dear God,
Thank you that you will always forgive us. Help us to forgive and love others in the same way, however hard that may be.
Amen.

Script for a class assembly based on assembly 24

suitable for Year Two

If the script is photocopied, the children's names can then be written to the left of the dialogue. Lots of children can have 'one-liners' to say (the narration); the two main parts go to the son (given in italic) and the father (given in bold). Add your own acting ideas.

Here is an umbrella.
Here is another umbrella.
You can use umbrellas for all sorts of things.
... rescuing cats if they are stuck up trees.
... carrying bags.
... getting changed behind on the beach.
... hiding under if it rains.
... playing snooker.
Jesus told a story about a young man who lived with his dad on a farm.
One day, the son decided he was going to find out what life was like in the big town nearby. He knew his dad was rich so he went to him and said,
Dad, give me my money. Now.
No please. No thank you.
Now, the father had a choice. Did he let his son go, or did he make him stay at home when he really didn't want to be there?

In the end he let him go.

So the son took his money, packed his bags, took his umbrella and off he went.

He might have gone to the races. His umbrella would have been very useful for sitting on.

He probably lost lots of money, but it didn't matter. He still had loads and loads of money.

More than likely he bought lots of new clothes. You needn't look while he gets changed because he'll nip behind his umbrella.

There again, he could have used his umbrella to pull some of his mates out of the river.

And as for the food the cook dished up… well, that had to be seen to be believed!

And then one day, his money ran out. It didn't run out of the door or anything like that. It was just that there was none left.

And suddenly he had no friends left, either. The whole lot left him and, just to make matters worse, there wasn't much food around either.

There was only one thing for it. He had to find a job. But what?

In the end he found one, looking after a load of pigs. Sitting all day watching pigs snort and roll in the mud and cough and trot and waddle.

And his umbrella?

Well, he turned it upside down and took some of the pigs' food home with him to eat.

This was the boy who had once had everything. And look at him now.

Well, after a while, he thought to himself,

All my father's workers have more than they can eat, and here am I about to starve. I will get up and go to my father and say, 'Father I have sinned against God and against you. Don't call me your son, treat me as one of your servants.'

That was brave of him. He's going to go back to his father; not as his father's son but as a servant.

Can you imagine it? This boy's been used to having everything done for him and he's going to ask to be a servant. So he set off. It was a long way. What he did not know was that his father was looking for him, longing for his son to appear.

And today was the day he had been waiting for.

Whahay, he's here!

the father shouted. Or something like that, we don't know for sure, but we do know he raced down the road to meet him.

But I've done wrong,

the boy said.

Treat me like a servant from now on.

No! You've come home. I thought you were dead, but you're alive. I thought you were lost, but you're found. You've come back to me. Let's celebrate!

And that was what they did. They partied.

And the father and the son stood together beneath an umbrella once more.

That story was first told in the Bible, apart from the umbrella because umbrellas had not been invented then, as far as we know.

Here are some things to think about.

The father wanted his son to come home because he loved him so much. He forgave and forgot about everything the son had done.

Christians believe that God is like that. It doesn't matter what we've done wrong, he will always forgive us if we ask him to.

Let's pray...

Dear God,

Thank you that you will always forgive us. Help us to forgive and love others in the same way, however hard that may be.

Amen.

The Lord's Prayer

Jesus' special prayer

Children will...

- think about different things people say to each other
- look at the Lord's Prayer in Matthew 6:9–13
- read the Lord's Prayer slowly and gain some understanding about what it means

You'll need...

- OHP and acetate of the Lord's Prayer
- paper and felt-tip pens or board to write on

Introduction...

Ask the children what they might say if they:

- wanted to show someone they thought they were special
- wanted good things to happen to everyone
- were hungry
- were sorry about something they had done
- were going somewhere new and wanted to be looked after

Write the children's suggestions down.

Story...

When Jesus was living on earth, someone asked him what people should say when they pray. Jesus gave his friends a special prayer which is called the Lord's Prayer.

(Use the OHP to work down the lines. This version of the Lord's Prayer is from the Contemporary English Version (CEV) of the Bible, and is found in Matthew 6:9–13.)

Our Father in heaven, help us to honour your name.
(Ask the children what heaven is (where God lives) and what 'honouring God's name' means (keeping it special). Refer back to ideas the children had in the Introduction.)
Come and set up your kingdom, so that everyone on earth will obey you, as you are obeyed in heaven.
(God is like a king who wants only good things to happen. Refer back to the children's second suggestion from the Introduction.)
Give us our food for today.
(Refer to third suggestion.)
Forgive us for doing wrong, as we forgive others.
(God wants us to be at peace with everyone. Refer to the fourth suggestion.)
Keep us from being tempted and protect us from evil.
(Refer to the fifth suggestion, then recap the whole prayer.)

Thinking time...

Think about one thing you can remember from the Lord's Prayer. How many other things can you remember? Which is the most important to you – to make God special, to want good things to happen, for everyone to have enough food, to be friends with everyone or to be kept safe?

Prayer...

Read the Lord's Prayer slowly, as given above.

Add. For thine is the Kingdom the power and the glory. For ever & ever Amen.

When we're in difficulty

26

Jesus calms a storm

Children will...

- look at weather symbols
- take part in acting out the story of Jesus calming the storm as in Matthew 8:23–27 and Mark 4:35–41
- think about the 'storms' people go through and who can help them

You'll need...

- photocopied weather symbols from page 112
- flip chart or OHP to write on

Introduction...

Look at **weather symbols** and talk about different types of **weather**.

Story...

Jesus was ever so tired. His friends suggested they went for a boat ride on the sea to get away from everyone so that Jesus could have a rest. It was evening and must have been getting dark.

Jesus' friends were fishermen. Their boat would have had a sail and oars. The Bible tells us that Jesus fell asleep in the back of the boat.

(All the children make gentle wave movements with their hands.)

That was what the sea was like: calm and gentle. There might have been a little breeze, but everything was peaceful.

But not for long. The Sea of Galilee is famous for its storms. They suddenly appear as if from nowhere. And that is exactly what happened on this evening. A fierce storm hit the lake.

(The children respond to the changes in weather as they continue to make wave movements.)

Suddenly, there was water everywhere: in the boat, under the boat, and above the boat. The wind and rain grew louder and stronger.

(Ask the children to make the sounds of the storm – slapping knees for rain, making 'whoooooo' sounds for the wind, rocking from side to side for the motion of the boat.)

Well, Jesus' friends thought the boat was going to sink, and do you know what Jesus was still doing? *(Sleeping!)*

Jesus' friends crawled along the bottom of the boat and shook him until he was awake.

What do you think they said to him? *('Save us!'; 'We are about to die!'; 'Don't you care we're about to die?')*

And Jesus sat up and asked them, 'Why are you so frightened? Don't you trust me?' He must have had to shout over the noise of the wind and the waves smashing against the side of the boat.

(Repeat what Jesus said, shouting it out.)

How do you think the friends felt when he said that? *(Awkward, silly, annoyed.)*

And then Jesus did something that could have been dangerous. He stood up. Right in the middle of the storm with the waves and the wind and the water and the rocking boat and the terrified friends watching him.

He didn't shout. He spoke in his normal voice, looking around and up as he spoke to the wind.

'Be quiet!' he said. Then he looked down at the waves. 'Be still!'

And the wind died down and there was a great calm. Stillness.

Do you know what the friends thought? They were afraid. Frightened. 'Who is this man?' they whispered to each other. 'Even the winds and waves obey him.'

Thinking time...

Ask the children to think of a time when everything was calm and happy. Then ask them to think of a time when life is like a storm. It might have been when something sad happened, or when they moved house, or when a pet died. It could be a time when they were very worried.
Who can help when there's a storm?

Prayer...

Dear God,
You know what it's like to be in a storm and you know that your friends were ever so scared. If we get scared about anything, help us to know that you are always with us.
Amen.

Training for life

27

Jesus' story about building houses on rock and on sand

This assembly can be linked to sports events.

Children will...

- think about how athletes train
- take part in the parable of the wise and foolish house builders in Matthew 7:24–27
- think about how to build firm foundations in their own lives

You'll need...

- sand
- rocks

Introduction...

Talk about **athletes** or footballers and how they have to **train** their bodies to be really fit. Ask some children to demonstrate exercises and see if they know how athletes train their bodies. (*Eating the right things, lots of sleep, exercise, help from trainers, sacrifice, dedication.)*

Story...

Jesus told a story about two men who were in a bit of a race. They were both going to build themselves a house. They had to choose which sort of land to build their houses on. They could either build on sand or on hard rocks. Which material would you choose? Why?

Well, the first man set off. He was a bit like an athlete who knows about getting fit and looking after himself, and he knew that rocks would be hard work to build on, but better in the end. So he started digging deep down into the ground. Then he laid the foundations and built upwards. He knew that would make the house very strong.

But it was hard work.

(Ask some children to pretend to dig, carry bricks and earth around the room, drag wood and put up doors. Keep emphasising all the hard work that is going in to the house.)

Meanwhile, the second man decided to build his house. He did not know about getting fit and looking after himself so he looked for the easiest place to build his house.

He decided to build on sand because there was no digging. He could start building straight away and before long his house was finished, too.

And then the storm came.

(Ask the children to make the storm, slapping their knees for rain, puffing for the wind, rocking to show the power of the storm.)

The rivers overflowed and the wind blew hard against the two houses. It was as if the wind and the rain were having a race too, to see which of them could knock the houses over first.

And the first one to fall was… the house built on the sand.

Thinking time...

Jesus said that the house built on the rocks is like people who think about their lives, like an athlete who trains and does what is right. The house built on the sand is like someone who does not think about what will happen to them in the future.

Which man are you being in each of these situations?

- when you can't be bothered to work hard at school.
- when you stop yourself saying something nasty about someone.
- when you do something to help someone else.
- when you push to the front of a queue.

How can you build your life carefully?

Prayer...

Dear God,
Help us to be like the man who built his house on the rock and build our lives carefully.
Amen.

Picnic time

Jesus feeds 5,000 people

Children will...

- talk about picnics
- hear about Jesus' picnic from John 6:1–14
- think about what God has provided for them and how to look after it

You'll need...

- some food to put in a lunch box
- five fish (fish fingers would do, or a fish-shaped piece of card)
- two loaves of bread (rolls or a bread-shaped piece of card)
- tea towel

Introduction...

Talk about what people take when they go on a **picnic**. Pack the lunch box with your items as you talk.

Story...

Jesus went on a picnic, but he didn't take any food with him. The five thousand people who came to listen to him talk did not have much food with them, either. Five thousand. That's an awful lot of people.

The crowd had been with Jesus for quite a while when the sun began to set. Jesus' friends must have thought everyone would start to go home. But they didn't. They stayed to listen to Jesus talk.

Now, Jesus' friends were quite good at noticing things. One of them came over to Jesus and caught his eye.

'It's late,' he said. 'This is a lonely place. Send the people away and let them go to the villages to buy food for themselves.'

If you were a baker and five thousand people turned up at your shop and asked to buy some bread, what would be the problem? *(Not enough bread, shop shut, you are asleep, you've been listening to Jesus anyway.)*

Jesus said to his friends, 'They don't have to leave.'

Now, that's given the friends a problem. They've got five thousand people and those people are getting hungry and tired. What will Jesus say now?

'Give them something to eat.'

'What? Us?'

'Yes, you.'

It so happened there was one boy there that day who had some food with him. One of Jesus' friends came across this boy and saw what he had. Five loaves and two fish.

Jesus' friend didn't grab the food off the boy. He went and told Jesus what the boy had.

'Then bring the loaves and fish to me,' Jesus said.

(Take out the loaves and fish wrapped up in a tea towel and hold them up.)

Jesus asked everyone to sit down on the grass. Then he took the five loaves and two fish, looked up to heaven, and gave thanks to God. He broke the loaves and gave them to the friends.

Now, the friends' eyes must have been wide open in amazement, because as Jesus broke the bread it just got bigger again. And the more he broke it the more there was. The same thing happened with the fish. On and on and on and on and on and on.

And the friends gave the bread and the fish out to the crowd of people. Everyone ate and had enough. The Bible says they even collected up twelve baskets of food that was left over afterwards. It was a real miracle. Something only God could do.

Thinking time...

Christians believe God knows what each one of us needs and looks after us.
What sort of things do we need? *(Material, emotional, families, friends, school.)*
What is the best thing you have ever been given?
The boy could have kept his food to himself, but he didn't. He shared it with everyone else. Ask the children what they could share with others. Maybe it is just a smile to someone who is unhappy, or saying something kind to someone who is upset. That's a good sort of thing to share.

Prayer...

Dear God,
Thank you for the way you look after us. Thank you for all the things you have given us. Help us look after them properly and be prepared to share them with others.
Amen.

Loving other people like ourselves

29

Jesus' teaching

Children will...

- think about their reactions to different situations
- consider Jesus' teaching based on Luke 10:27
- think about how they should react to different situations

You'll need...

- coats and other dressing up clothes

Introduction...

Ask a child to put on a coat/item of **clothing**. Where might he/she be going dressed in those clothes?
Examples of clothes and scenarios:

- shopping
- party
- school
- football match

Story...

In the Bible, Jesus says we should love our neighbours just like we love ourselves.

(Ask children to dress up and act out one of the scenarios given below. After each one, ask how the person who was dressed up was showing love to someone else.)

1 You go shopping and see someone fall over. What do you do?
OR
You go shopping and see a little boy who is lost. What do you do?
2 You go to a party and two of your friends fall out. What do you do?
OR
You go to a party and the friend you went with doesn't feel very well. What do you do?
3 You are at school and someone says something nasty to your friend. What do you do?
OR
You are at school and the person you sit next to forgets her pencils. What do you do?
4 You go to a football match and your little brother is scared of the crowd. What do you do?
OR
You go to a football match and your dad sits next to your little sister but he can't sit next to you as well. What do you do?

Thinking time...

Think of a time when you showed love to someone and helped them. What did it feel like? What happened?

Prayer...

Dear God,
It's easy to look after ourselves and sometimes it's hard to look after other people. Please help us do what is right.
Amen.

Moving on

Jesus' trust in God to be with him wherever he went

This assembly can be linked in with the end of the school year or when children are leaving the safety of a known environment.

Children will...

- think about how they have to 'move on' as they get older
- consider how Jesus' trust in his father helped him to move on
- think positively about moving on

You'll need...

- multi-link cubes
- blown up photocopies of pictures on pages 126–128

Introduction...

Ask several children to hold up **shapes** made from multi-link cubes and introduce the idea that each shape represents a different group of people they belong to. For example; school, class, Cubs, Rainbows, swimming lessons, families.

Story...

Jesus belonged to different groups as well. Here are his best friends, his disciples. *(Show the relevant picture and put it by one of the multi-link shapes.)* Jesus spent a lot of time with his friends. What kind of things did Jesus do with his friends?

(Give the children clues, either by acting the scenes out or by giving verbal clues to some of the things Jesus did with his disciples. For example, having a barbecue breakfast on the beach, going through a storm in a boat, talking with them, eating meals, healing people.)

Jesus had other friends as well. Just outside Jerusalem is a place called Bethany. Jesus had some very special friends who lived there, called Mary, Martha and Lazarus. *(Put the appropriate label on another multi-link shape.)*

Then there were those who came to listen to him, and there were those who came to him because they wanted him to make them better if they were ill.

(Put appropriate label in place on another multi-link shape and ask one or two children to act out someone being healed and someone listening to Jesus.)

Jesus had his family as well. His mother, Mary, his earthly father, Joseph, and his brothers, James, Joseph, Simon and Judas. He had some sisters as well but the Bible does not tell us what their names were.

(Put appropriate label on the last shape then hold it up.)

This is where Jesus started off: as part of a family, just like you.

(Break off one of the multi-links and move it around the various multi-link shapes, representing other groups Jesus knew.)

Sometimes Jesus was with his friends, sometimes his family. Then he made some more friends and as he went from place to place, he belonged to different groups.

We belong to different groups, too. Sometimes it's hard to move on, sometimes it's easy.

Jesus trusted God that when he moved to a new group, God would look after him and help him make friends. That must have helped him a lot.

Thinking time...

Which groups do you belong to?
How long have you belonged to them?
Will you always belong to them or will you have to move on?
What can you do to help you move on without worrying?
If you are worried about moving on and finding a new group, who could you tell? Who could help you?

Prayer...

Dear God,
You know what it is like to have to move on because you did it when you lived on earth. Help us to trust that you will look after us wherever we go.
Amen.